RELIGIOUS AND MONASTIC LIFE EXPLAINED

REVEREND DOM PROSPER GUÉRANGER O.S.B.

AETERNA PRESS

PUBLISHED BY AETERNA PRESS.
COVER DESIGN BY AETERNA PRESS.

AUTHORIZED VERSION FROM THE FRENCH OF RT. REV. DOM PROSPER GUÉRANGER, O.S.B. ABBOT OF SOLESMES BY REV. JEROME VETH, O.S.B. CONCEPTION ABBEY, CONCEPTION, MO.

PUBLISHED BY B. HERDER, 17 SOUTH BROADWAY, ST. LOUIS, MO., 1908

SANDS & CO., LONDON AND EDINBURGH B. HERDER, FREIBURG (BADEN)

NIHIL OBSTAT. F. G. HOLWECK, CENSOR S. LUDOVICI, DIE 22. SEPT. 1908.

IMPRIMATUR. + JOHANNES J. GLENNON, ARCHEPISCOPUS S. LUDOVICI. S. LUDOVICI, DIE 23. SEPT. 1908.

ISBN-13: 978-1-78516-755-3

AVAILABLE AS AN E-BOOK:
WWW.AETERNAPRESS.COM

CONTENTS

PREFACE OF THE TRANSLATOR

In presenting this translation of that most valuable work, commonly known as "Réglement," from the prolific pen of the learned and ascetic Abbot Dom Prosper Guéranger, it is our aim to meet, to some extent, a long felt necessity and oft-expressed desire that it be made accessible to our English-speaking brethren. Though our labour may not be crowned with the same success as that of the renowned author, we hope, nevertheless, that this work will find a hearty welcome and approval. May God graciously accept it as an instrument for showering His richest blessings on all who faithfully seek Him in the religious state.

THE TRANSLATOR.

Conception, Mo., June 13, 1908.

Feast of St. Anthony.

PREFACE TO THE FRENCH EDITION

Many religious houses have requested us to communicate to them the instructions which Dom Guéranger left us for the training of novices. We do it willingly, convinced that these few pages may be studied with advantage.

FR. CHARLES COUTURIER

Abbot of Solesmes.

Solesmes, Feast of the Ascension, May 14, 1885.

CHAPTER I

ESSENCE OF THE RELIGIOUS LIFE

The religious life embraces three fundamental objects:

1. Penance for sins committed; wherefore it is called conversion.

2. The imitation of Jesus Christ by the fulfilment of His precepts and counsels; in consequence of which the religious becomes like to Him.

3. Union with God, even in this world, by Charity.

Now, this union cannot be reached until certain obstacles encountered in man are removed. They are of a threefold nature, namely, the attachment, lawful though it may be, to earthly possessions, which chains man to the goods of this world; the pleasures of the senses, which divide the heart of man between God and the creature; self-will, which disturbs the harmony between the will of God and the will of man. True renunciation by poverty of spirit and of deed removes the obstacle presented by the attachment to earthly possessions; perfect purity of body, heart and soul, that of sensual pleasures, and sincere obedience to the will of another as unto the will of God breaks the attachment to self-will.

The religious life is not a transient, but a permanent state. This poverty, chastity and obedience should, then, become, as it were, the second nature of the religious, and inseparable from him. Now, this is accomplished at the taking of the perpetual vows, which alone constitute one a member of the religious state.

Once having entered upon this permanent state of religion, man is bound to strive after perfection. Now perfection consists in the love of God, or charity; and charity unites the soul with God.

Religion likewise effects the imitation of Jesus Christ; for the entire life of our Saviour involves the three virtues which form the matter of the vows.

Religion, lastly, accomplishes most perfectly amendment of life and true penance in those who profess it, by opposing to the three ailments of sinful man three wholesome remedies, which being applied effect the atonement for sin as well as the acquisition of the virtues.

Such is the general idea you should have of the religious life. Ponder over it unceasingly, and behold in it the aim proposed at the beginning of the novitiate. And since you are about to embrace the religious life in its monastic form, it is important for you to become familiar with the rule of life according to which you desire to consecrate yourselves to God.

CHAPTER II

ESSENCE OF THE MONASTIC LIFE

The principal characteristics of monastic life are:

1. Separation from the world by the enclosure and the habit.
2. The daily solemnization of the Divine Office.
3. Work.
4. Mortification of the body.
5. Community life.
6. Works of zeal towards our neighbour (if obedience allows or demands them).

Having given this definition of monastic life, it will next be expedient to consider its different elements in particular, as also the manner of practically applying them in the novitiate.

1. Separation from the World.

The monastic life is, by its very nature, a retired life. Hence it requires of those who profess it that they live within the precincts of the monastery. The separation from the world should be the literal fulfilment of this word of our Lord Jesus Christ: "Everyone that hath left father or mother" and of that other one: "Come, follow me." This clearly shows that the monastic spirit is one of retirement, characterized by the religious enclosure.

The monastery must be considered the place of our sojourn until death. We should have such predeliction for this retirement that our love of the enclosure will not diminish when, after profession, obedience occasionally summons us to appear in the world.

Behold in the isolation from dear relatives, which will henceforth be your lot, the essential fulfilment of the counsel of Jesus Christ. This separation will be the touchstone of your vocation and also the matter of the sacrifice upon which the religious life rests as its foundation.

Though you have resolved to live away from your relatives, beware of the idea that a perfect religious must renounce all filial affection for them. On the contrary, purified by divine charity, this affection will only become the more active, tender and faithful. What is said here of one's family applies also to relations with friends left in the world, provided these bonds of friendship are honourable and virtuous.

Though you live shut up in the bosom of the novitiate, circumstances may demand a renewal of former ties. Each order has in this regard its special regulations which must be duly learned and observed.

The external enclosure avails but little, unless the spirit of the world be banished from the heart. Be intent, therefore, on blotting out all worldly memories; appraise all things according to the spirit of Religion which is opposed to the spirit of the world; shun all worldly manners, and observe, without affectation, that gravity and modesty of deportment becoming to the state you desire to embrace. In your intercourse with people of the world, you must take care not to lose your aversion to the spirit of the world; let your behaviour be edifying to everyone with whom you may come in contact.

Hold in great reverence the religious habit, which is the visible sign of separation from the world, and daily put it on with this sentiment. Be careful to keep it clean; never take it off without necessity, and always wear it when you appear outside of your cell.

2. Divine Service.

"Let naught be preferred to the work of God." It is in these words that our holy Father St. Benedict teaches us to look upon divine service as the noblest and most useful of our daily exercises. For it naturally follows, that he who has left all things for God should make it his first duty to give himself up to God.

Your fidelity to your vocation will justly be measured by your zeal for the divine service. This zeal will manifest itself not only in the choir service, but also in the care bestowed upon learning the rules of the Divine Office, the sacred chant and ceremonies.

Do not be satisfied with conscientiously carrying out the instructions of the rubrics and the text of the Breviary; let your pious attention embrace also the entirety of the Divine Office and thus render yourselves fit for its performance. The pitch and inflection of the voice and the manner of proceeding in all the general and particular ceremonies are also points for observation. Do not consider attention to these details a distraction, but often entreat God that you may acquit yourselves in His service with dignity, recollection, modesty and precision.

Apply yourselves with zeal to the sacred chant, seeking only the glory of God. Should you experience any prejudice against the sacred chant, do not yield to it; resist it manfully, and remember that God will exact an account of you in this respect. And even if you should not arrive at great perfection in this matter, the very thought of having prevented the disturbances always occasioned by an undisciplined voice will be of great consolation to you.

With regard to the readings in choir, let the quantity and accent of syllables be observed with exactness. Do not become discouraged if up to this time you have been neglectful of such an essential point.

Be always well prepared when you are about to participate in any sacred function, and your conscience will afterwards have no reason to accuse you for your short-comings in the presence of the Divine Majesty. Finally, be zealous in mastering every detail so that when, after your profession, you are called upon to fulfil the functions of hebdomadary, you may be a source of edification to all.

Neglect not the proper recollection before the Divine Office. Employ the moments at the so-called "station" in raising your hearts to God and in preparing yourselves to appear before Him. During the procession into the church, everything that may distract the recollected mind must be avoided. Having arrived at your place in choir, make the necessary preparations and thrust aside every thought not pertaining to the divine praise. Take proper notice of the sacred chant and ceremonies that you may be edified in them, avoiding at the same time all looks and motions which only distract you from the great object which should receive your full attention.

Let the different bows, viz., the simple, medium or moderate and profound, be made from deep religious feeling and not from mere habit. Do not fail, at the end of the psalms and hymns, to unite with the particular intention of adoring the Holy Trinity which is associated with the mystery celebrated or the Saint honoured on the day in question.

Once convinced that its familiar use will constitute a long step on the way to contemplation, we shall learn to appreciate the sacred psalmody which has been, as it were, the daily bread of the Saints of our holy Order. Let us, therefore, ask this grace of God and also that of understanding and relishing the other parts of the Divine Office.

When singing or reciting, you must lovingly penetrate into the sense of the words and make it your own. Note carefully the tender allusions used by our Holy Mother the Church in her liturgical formulas that you may be nourished by the hidden manna which strengthens the soul and endows it with understanding for the holy things of God. Gratefully call to mind, during the course of the day, the various impressions received on those occasions from the Holy Ghost that you may merit to receive new ones.

Whatever is sung or recited by the hebdomadary, especially the daily collect, to which we ought to have a particular devotion, should be followed with pious attention. Care must also be taken that the different bows at the Prayers and the other recitations be properly observed.

We must keep before us the fact that the Church constantly uses the chant at divine service to express the ardour of the sentiments produced in her by the Holy Ghost. From this we justly conclude that the disposition with which we ought to celebrate the Divine Office is that of holy enthusiasm for the sacred mysteries. Let us act in accordance with the word of our holy Father St. Benedict, who says that we should "assist at His (God's) praises in such a manner that heart and voice may accord."

Let us sing with interest, docility and humility, shunning everything that savours of effeminacy, vanity or caprice. Always bear in mind that the chant when disfigured by human presumption is not pleasing to God. Our song is destined to mingle with the angelic praises, and this thought will certainly be an incentive urging us to watch over nature during the performance of such a sacred function.

Let our esteem for the divine service to which we have pledged ourselves be increased, as this supreme homage to the Divine Majesty is less common in our days, on account of the violent and sacrilegious suppression of so many monasteries and convents whose walls once resounded with the holy praises. Often give thanks to God that He has chosen you to promote and transmit to posterity the traditions of public prayer, and ask Him with the Prophet that the voices of those who celebrate His holy name be heard and multiplied.

Let us shrink with horror from the worldly idea that the time passed in choir would be better employed in study or other exercises of piety; as if any work could be compared with the liturgical prayer in dignity, importance and efficacy; as if the prayer of the Church, offered up to God under conditions laid down by herself, were not, after the Holy Sacrifice and the administration of the Sacraments, the most profitable and holy work performed on earth.

Far from entertaining such unworthy notions which savour of a dangerous materialism, let us rather deplore our inability to imitate the holy fervour of our forefathers who rose for divine service at midnight and prolonged the office of the day far beyond our strength.

Let this consideration stimulate us zealously to execute whatsoever the Constitutions prescribe concerning the Divine Office and endure with joy the blessed hardships which may at times be exacted from us during the celebration of the great ceremonies.

3. Monastic Work.

The monastic life rests on divine service and work as on two hinges. By the former we devote ourselves to God; by the latter we meritoriously occupy those hours which our frail spirits do not allow us to devote to contemplation.

Monastic work, therefore, is an homage paid to God; for this very reason it should be commenced with prayer and carried on in the spirit of prayer. Hence, cherish great affection for this fundamental principle of our calling, and realize that the monk should always be found seriously occupied, the hours of recreation excepted. And even these serve only to render the soul more disposed for further prayer and work.

You must acquire now, for all your life time, the habit of fleeing from idleness which is, as our holy Patriarch tells us, the enemy of the soul. Above all things, do not surrender yourselves to empty imaginations which enervate the mind and deaden the senses for what is holy. Remember that diligent work abates the passions and prevents a multitude of sins. Offering up to God all your moments, you will secure final perseverance and acquire an immense amount of merit. If it be somewhat hard for you to submit to labour, rouse yourselves by the thought that it is a punishment imposed on sinful man by the Almighty. You will then gather sufficient strength to accept it with a humble and heroic heart, as our first parents received this sentence from their Creator. Consider that the Son of God assumed our human nature to set us the example and to make us understand that work is one of the first duties of man and a powerful means of reparation.

In order that our work may be meritorious and truly religious, it must conform to the dictates of obedience. Natural inclination and human fancy may also produce deeds praised and esteemed by men; but such deeds will not find an eternal reward on the day of retribution. Therefore, let most perfect obedience accompany all your works; follow most minutely the plan laid out for the proper use of your time, and do nothing beyond it without previous permission.

If the work enjoined happen to correspond with your anticipation, sanctify this attraction by frequently offering it up to God that He may graciously work in and by you. If the work be less inviting, then remember that one of the aims pursued in religious life is to break with self-will; that it is always better and safer to counteract than to follow this attraction.

Nor forget that you must perform the work for the glory of God, who will some day repay it with interest. Take heed that you do not acquit yourself of this duty as a hireling, but prove, by your zeal, that you really seek God in this second means of the religious state. Thus you shall obtain the assistance of God and often find your zeal blessed from on high and rewarded with unexpected progress.

We distinguish two kinds of monastic work: mental and manual. The first is the more excellent when directed towards a supernatural end and regulated by obedience; the second is also of great value, because it humbles the pride of man and consecrates the body to the service of God.

You will be employed in both, but especially in mental work. Let all your studies and your reading ultimately aim at advancement in the knowledge of God and His mysteries, the love of holy Church and the acquisition of those virtues which are most essential to the religious. With the will thus disposed, mental work will undoubtedly be most profitable for your spiritual welfare.

You will, on the other hand, submit also to manual labour. For you will be indiscriminately appointed to the more lowly services of the house, as sweeping, helping in the kitchen, working in the garden, etc. Father Master will determine the time for such work and whether you work together or each one for himself.

4. Mortification of the Body.

Mortification of the body is another essential element and principal characteristic of the monastic life. Hold it, therefore, in great esteem, convinced that a rule which lacks this element, however excellent it may be otherwise, cannot claim a place among the monastic rules.

Recall to memory the mortified life of St. John the Baptist, the austerities of the Fathers of the desert, the life of our holy Patriarch and the other Saints of our Order, and you will be more and more confirmed in the conviction that the struggle against the flesh by means of bodily mortification is a prime factor of the monk's life.

This conviction will be strengthened the more one considers the necessity of reparation for the sinner who enters the monastery with the special purpose of working out the amendment of his life; the great help which is gained by the soul in humiliating the flesh; the vanity of those who, contrary to the example of the Saints, pretend to arrive at spiritual mortification without employing bodily chastisement, and, lastly, the inestimable advantage of participating in the bodily and mental sufferings of our Lord Jesus Christ.

Such thoughts as these make it easy to recognize the wisdom of the penitential practices which our holy Patriarch has established in the holy Rule, especially fasting and abstinence from flesh-meat. And since these venerable and salutary prescriptions have been modified by holy Church, making allowance for our weakness, we will adhere the more energetically to what is left us of these holy practices.

Veneration for these precious remnants of the ancient observance should manifest itself in every way possible and should inspire us to bear the burden they impose with resolute endurance and the utmost precision. Let the novices always speak of them respectfully and support one another by setting the example of observing them faithfully. Should their health demand some indulgence at the beginning, they will avail themselves, in simplicity of heart, of such as may be granted and ask God to give them more strength that soon they too may join their brethren in this holy work.

As for such bodily works of mortification as are not prescribed by the Constitutions, none shall be practised of one's own accord or without the special permission of the Father Master.

Let the thought of mortification stimulate you to suffer without complaint, even contentedly and with cheerfulness, the inconveniences resulting from the inclemency of the seasons, from coarse diet or its defective preparation, from less comfortable lodging, from sickness and indisposition or from the observance of the rule. But if, nevertheless, you have reason to think that your health should be taken into consideration, then you should inform Father Master. This being done, leave the whole matter in the hands of God, accepting with equanimity the alleviation granted - or continuing to bear with good will the yoke of the religious life, should it not be thought proper to yield to your weakness.

5. Community Life.

The monastic life is a life in common. The spirit of God has designed it thus that the monk may find a powerful help in the example of his fellow-religious and acquire a high degree of merit in the exercise of fraternal charity.

This being the case, regard with reverence the family life which you are called upon to lead. Learn to appreciate its advantages and promote its spirit in yourselves and others. Rejoice at seeing others participate in the favours of which you are the special object, and love one another as brethren who have been called together by the same vocation. Take pleasure in the company of your brethren, because the Holy Ghost Himself has chosen and united you for one and the same end. Let the joys, as well as the afflictions, be in common, and let your familiar intercourse preserve intact the mutual respect which is due.

Encourage one another in perseverance and progress, and offer up your fervent prayers for those brethren who labour under temptation or trial. Studiously avoid every word or expression that might in any way be offensive to your brethren or induce them to relax their efforts to attain the perfection to which all ought to aspire.

Besides cherishing an interior affection for one another, show also by outward acts that you are united by mutual charity. Endeavour always to vie with one another in politeness, conceding mutually in word and deed and detesting whatever savours of selfishness.

Those who have been honoured by admission to Holy Orders, will always recollect their own unworthiness of such a sublime dignity, and never exalt themselves above others who have not yet received this favour.

God often permits religious vocation to bring together persons of quite opposite natural dispositions. Therefore, let us be on our guard against every form of antipathy which the devil may endeavour to enkindle by means of these differences. Use all your energy to overcome every feeling of antipathy and, at the same time, take care not to yield to those blind and purely natural attractions by which you would become attached to this or that one of your brethren in particular. Moreover, be ever careful to correct whatever might possibly injure the family spirit, which should be the common bond of all.

Should anyone perceive in himself a tendency towards isolation, that source of misanthropy which can so soon render community life loathsome, let him not yield to this dangerous temptation. Such a one must summon all his willpower to overcome it at the very outset by prayer and also by repeated and persevering efforts, lest this disposition should awaken in him a spirit of pride and expose him to the danger of losing his vocation.

The family spirit will inspire the novices to be frankly subject to their Reverend Father Master, who, as their chief and guide, is the immediate bond of unity of their society. Let them manifest due respect for the monks, in comparison with whom they are children and should see in everyone of them a father and cherish filial affection towards the Abbot, as Christ's representative in the monastery.

Cultivate, too, sincere attachment to our Order. Incessantly beseech our Lord to protect, maintain and increase it for His glory and for the welfare and the sanctification of souls. Do not undervalue the mode of life pursued therein. It is recognized and approved by the Apostolic See as being in conformity with the spirit of St. Benedict. Consequently, this mode of life justly claims the respect of all the children of the Church; how much more should it be reverenced by those whom divine grace has led to the novitiate.

Never allow yourselves, under the pretext that they are followed more exactly elsewhere, the least criticism concerning the manner of observing the rules. Remember that a novice has not yet taken upon himself any obligation and is therefore at liberty to direct his steps whithersoever his inclination may lead him. But if some should not feel any attraction towards the Order, its spirit or its administration, let it be understood that for them community life will be unbearable. It is the duty of such to withdraw from a mode of life which will never gain the allegiance of their thoughts and intentions.

This family spirit, founded on our relations to Divine Providence, should not lessen in us due appreciation of the other Rules and Constitutions approved by the Holy See.

Far from harbouring any prejudice against them, let us fervently pray for the preservation and extension of all the various religious Orders, take a lively interest in their progress and sympathize with them when pressed by misfortune.

6. Works of Zeal for our Neighbour.

Although one of the essentials of monastic life is separation from the world, we must, nevertheless, beware of the idea that the monk may possibly arrive at the perfection proper to his state without including zeal for his neighbour in his intentions and mode of life. "And He" (the Lord), says Ecclesiasticus (xvii, 12), "gave to every one of them commandment concerning his neighbour." Monastic life tends to draw man nearer to God by submission and love. So the monk, entering into the spirit of his vocation, should be carried away by a holy zeal for the welfare of his neighbour, the great and eternal occupation of God, for which end He delivered up even His only-begotten Son.

Let no one imagine that monastic life consists exclusively in working out our own perfection, regardless of the sanctification of our neighbour. Let us rather bear in mind that the good works performed in the Church affect the entire mystic body of Jesus Christ, in consequence of the communion of Saints. Accordingly, the intentions of each one of the faithful ought to extend beyond his own person. From its very institution, the religious state was particularly destined by our Lord to become, as regards its merits, a treasury of good works for all, and the Divine Office, which forms the chief work of the monk, bestows on him the function of a universal intercessor. In one word, nothing can be more contrary to charity, which is the distinguishing mark of every true disciple of Christ, than a petty occupation with self, which would conceal from the eyes of the monk the needs of those who will always remain his brethren.

Let us, therefore, constantly long for the kingdom of God, the immediate object of the second petition in the Lord's Prayer. This petition includes also the conversion of Jews and infidels, the return of schismatics and heretics, the repentance of sinners, the perseverance of the just and the perfection of those souls which are called by God to a closer union with Him even in this world. These considerations enable us to observe how often we ourselves have been aided and advanced by others in the work of our conversion. Being still supported by them in our progress, we would do wrong in yielding to selfish indifference and in looking at things from a point of view which is not that of God. All our desires, intentions, prayers, penitential and religious works should be offered up to God in a spirit of zeal and charity for our neighbour. Faithfully fostered in us, this sentiment will preserve us from that cold and indifferent spirit with which the world so often reproaches the inmates of religious institutions.

You must not, however, limit yourselves to hidden and interior conviction. Exercise, from the very beginning of the novitiate, as far as circumstances permit, apostolic zeal, cheering one another by your good example, behaviour and conversation, by labouring for the maintenance and development of the religious spirit and confirming those who might waver in their vocation. As to your relatives and friends in the world, you should resolve, according to the degree of intercourse that will be granted you, to encourage them in the right and induce them to abandon any evil or error into which they may unhappily have been led.

Husband the time before your holy profession and prepare yourselves well for those works of zeal which may be entrusted to you by obedience, be they employments within the monastery, or works which have for their object the propagation of the truth in writings destined for the public, or the exercise of the sacred ministry, preaching the word of God and administering the sacraments, having always the desire that these various means may promote the glory of God and the salvation and sanctification of souls. But if only a small share of these works be allotted to you, or even if obedience should not call you to that field, still resolve to contribute to the welfare of souls at least by leading an edifying life, which will always be of great benefit to Christian society. For the sight of a monastery wherein God is served with fervour is in itself an eloquent sermon and a powerful promoter of the supernatural element in every country.

Actuated by motives of this kind, we will magnanimously recommend to God the works of zeal performed in our Order. Let us often entreat Him to accept our endeavours, whether they regard our own deeds or those of the public, or serve directly the sublime object of the salvation of souls. Ask Him frequently that for His divine glory and service our Order may be filled with men powerful in word and deed, men after the pattern of the many illustrious Saints of the monastic life, who became all things to all men and knew so well how to serve the Church and the souls ransomed by Jesus Christ. The whole life of these great religious souls was, at the same time, the most vivid expression of the spirit which our great Patriarch has laid down in his holy Rule.

In conclusion, let it be remarked that zeal for our neighbour should excite in us tender compassion for the suffering souls in Purgatory. Do not forget that the Church suffering owes the immense relief which is yearly sent her on the second day of November from the Church militant to the Abbey of Cluny, but heartily preserve this holy tradition by using every means to succour these souls so dear to God; for having sealed their earthly career, they long intensely for the efficacious help which the Divine Mercy empowers us to render them.

CHAPTER III

ON THE EXCELLENCE AND OBSERVATION OF THE RULE

Having explained the essential features of the monastic life, we must now instruct the novice on the excellence of the Rule, in order to inspire him with the respect which it deserves. This will be easily gained by considering that the man consecrated to God needs a support for his weakness in the struggle to live up to the requirements of the religious life in general and the monastic life in particular. It must also be remembered that to monks who live together as one society, common and definite laws are indispensable for the maintenance of order and the attainment of the object of the cenobitic life.

To satisfy this double want, in the course of time many religious rules have come into existence. Such great importance is attached to them by the Church, that she first ascertains and confirms its rule before she approves any religious society. Hence the custom of our times that the religious not only professes the three vows essential to his state, but also promises to live according to a certain rule approved by the Church. From this it follows that the life of a religious cannot be perfectly acceptable to God, unless it agrees in all things with the rule according to which he took his vows. The monk whose life is in constant opposition to the rule cannot flatter himself that he is on the straight road to heaven.

Let the novice, then, learn the true value of the Rule and apply himself with diligence and understanding to its practice even in the novitiate. It makes the religious pleasing to God by fortifying him against his weakness and prompting him to undertake a number of supernatural works which would scarcely have been performed otherwise. Lastly, it secures in the community the order without which it would not exist for any length of time in an edifying condition.

By the rule we mean not only the holy Rule of our Blessed Father St. Benedict, but also the Statutes approved by the Holy See which adapt the holy Rule to our circumstances without, however, altering its spirit and, lastly, the regulations and ordinances made by the legitimate authority in accordance with the Rule and the Statutes.

Behold in the holy Rule the testament of our holy Patriarch and the most precious legacy we have from him. Treat with respect the volume in which it is contained and listen devoutly to its reading in the Chapter and the Refectory. Memorize it cheerfully to the extent imposed upon you and be attentive in the fear of the Lord to the explanations and commentaries you receive in the instructions of the novitiate or in spiritual conferences.

There cannot be the least doubt that one of our principal sources of grace is to be found in mastering this truly admirable book, which has made so many Saints and which is stamped with the spirit of God. God alone could have inspired our great Patriarch with the charity, wisdom, mildness and force which excites our admiration in every line. If in our age there is no longer a literal observance of its precepts, we should at least lack none of its spirit; moreover, where our authorized practice is less severe, we should enter the more into the intentions of our holy Patriarch by accomplishing the little we do in such a manner that he may always acknowledge us as his children. It is through the Rule of St. Benedict that we are Benedictines; therefore, we must try, by every means in our power, to identify ourselves with it and imbue the work of our entire life with its spirit.

The Statutes, which have for their principal object the adaptation of the holy Rule to the moral and physical decline of the present generation, should also be held in sovereign respect by the novice, who ought to become well acquainted with them and observe them exactly.

But since it is necessary to state the precise extent of the obligations which you are called upon to assume, it is well to note the following: with the exception of those articles of the holy Rule and the Statutes which bear upon the matter of the vows or are at the same time established in Canon Law, the different precepts contained in the said holy Rule or Statutes are not obliging in themselves under sin. This generally accepted opinion agrees with the teaching of St. Thomas and saves us from overburdening the Conscience with a heavy yoke. It must not be forgotten, on the other hand, that any violation of the different points of the holy Rule and Statutes which proceeds from a feeling of contempt or is accompanied by scandal becomes a sin, mortal or venial, according to the degree of the contempt or the scandal.

Although you are, as novices, not yet under the obligation of the Rule or the vows, you should, nevertheless, accustom yourselves to the divers practices of the observance as if you were already bound by your profession. If his bodily or spiritual welfare demand it, greater indulgence may be granted to the postulant until he is somewhat accustomed to his surroundings. Too abrupt a transition from one mode of life to the other must be avoided. But the novice should conform to the letter of the common and particular observances of the professed and be happy to give God this proof of fidelity to his vocation.

Moreover, remember that a novice who is ungenerous or unfaithful in observing the rule runs the risk of not being permitted to make his profession; and even were he admitted to the religious state, he would still have incurred the most serious responsibility of having neglected the means of pursuing the vocation pointed out by God, which is one of the greatest dangers that our salvation may meet with in this world.

The thought that the bad example which he sets by violating the rule may be imitated by his brethren should also deter him from deserting the path of duty. To sum up, let everyone contribute to the common edification by preparing himself for a holy profession by perfect fidelity in all things.

CHAPTER IV

ON THE ESSENTIAL FOUNDATION OF RELIGIOUS LIFE

Having acquainted you with the essential notions of monastic life, we must now resume the contemplation of religious life, which finds in the former its most excellent and complete form. Religious life consists, as you know, in the practice of the three virtues of poverty, chastity and obedience, by means of which the soul disengages itself from the obstacles which arrest its march to perfection; purifies itself from its stains by expiation, and arrives at union with God by the imitation of Jesus Christ. This state, we maintain, must be firmly established, otherwise it cannot endure. Now, the foundation on which it must be established is the Christian life, which necessarily precedes the religious life, and is so indispensable that the latter, even though its outward appearance might, perchance, be retained for some time, inevitably falls with the former.

The Christian life consists chiefly in these two things: the presence of sanctifying grace in the soul and the practice of the precepts of our Lord Jesus Christ.

Without sanctifying grace, the soul is dead to God and to itself; in the state of sanctifying grace, it possesses life. It would, therefore, be vanity for a religious who is not in the state of sanctifying grace to imagine that he is fulfilling the obligations of his vocation, even if he tries to be faithful in the practice of the vows and the rule. The whole would lack its foundation. If he should fail to abandon this unhappy state promptly, he would run the risk of eternal damnation, the more so in as much as he had been favoured with a more holy calling. From this it follows that the religious is under the same, nay, even greater obligations than the simple Christian to flee sin, which dispels grace, and that he cannot rely on the holy exercises of his state of life. He must often consider his frailty and the deep malice with which the evil spirits are wont to attack the servants of God. Let him remember that it is written: "He that thinketh himself to stand, let him take heed lest he fall." (I Cor. x, 12.) Following the counsels of Jesus Christ, he should watch and pray that he enter not into temptation; lastly he must fear and shun the occasions which he knows to be hurtful, roused to the combat by the thought that, no matter how great the merits acquired by a religious may be, it needs only one mortal sin to deprive him, in an instant, of all the graces accumulated throughout long years of toil.

The religious differs from the Christian in the world, as to the care which he should bestow upon the preservation of sanctifying grace, only in so far that one mortal sin would plunge him into a state much more deplorable, because he has more at stake than the simple faithful and misuses a greater number of graces.

And since deliberate and habitual venial sin makes the danger imminent of falling into mortal sin, it is necessary that the religious, even more than the simple Christian, should watch over his conscience in regard to venial sin, lest he diminish, by his infidelities, the abundance of actual grace, the need of which is felt at every moment, and lose gradually his sense of the inestimable value of sanctifying grace.

Second only to this supreme good, which has been purchased with the blood of Jesus Christ, are the precepts of our Lord. Since religious life is the perfection of Christianity, and the Christian life as we have said consists in the observance of the precepts of Jesus Christ, therefore endeavour to keep them with ever-growing fidelity. Beware of the delusion into which so many have fallen of persuading themselves that a religious can be held irreproachable as such without being blameless as a Christian. Examine yourselves often to discover whether the efforts you put forth in order to acquire the special qualities of the monk do not remove from your view the obligation of maintaining and developing by grace those qualities which constitute one a true follower of Christ. For this purpose mark well the chapter of the holy Rule entitled "Quae sunt instrumenta bonorum operum," wherein our holy Patriarch seems to blend into one all the precepts of the Decalogue and the holy Gospel, together with the counsels of perfection.

The theological and moral virtues should be daily cultivated by the religious with ever increasing attention. On these virtues would have rested the hope of his salvation, had he remained in the world; salvation knows no different conditions in the religious state.

Let these virtues, then, be the prime matter of your daily self-examinations and your chief care when you approach the sacrament of Penance. The more you endeavour to acquire, establish and augment in your soul the Christian virtues, the greater will be your desire for religious perfection. What else is amendment of life, which must be the special object of your profession, but the strenuous effort to model your life after the precepts of Jesus Christ, by planting the virtues recommended by the Church?

Hence, let the Christian life be considered the preamble to the religious life and its indispensable support. As the impregnable foundation for the Christian life, first of all, should be established the fear of the Lord, which is, as the royal Prophet tells us (Ps. cx. 10), "the beginning of wisdom." The effeminate spirit of our age would provide for the sinner a quite different foundation for the service of God. But what fallacy this is! No doubt, it is written that love dispels fear, but who can be sure that he possesses perfect love? And even if love does dispel fear, is this not a proof that fear must exist before love? May you, therefore, be able to grasp, in its fullness, what our holy Patriarch teaches us on this subject, and equip yourselves, for your whole life, with this salutary fear, which is a solid basis for the amendment of our lives and the best preservative against the decline of religion.

Do not shrink from meditating on death, the inevitable end of this life, the hour of which is uncertain, which comes closer upon us every moment and which shall establish us forever in the one eternity or the other. Watch in expectation of the judgment of God, when fidelity in our works shall be our only defence; a judgment, whose sentence shall be irrevocable and without appeal. Reflect frequently upon the eternal pains of hell and the vain despair of those who are consumed by its everlasting flames. Fathom the abyss of the justice of God, which did not spare his own Son, when He took upon himself our sins. Be ever mindful of the warning of our Redeemer on his way to Calvary: "If in the green wood they do these things, what shall be done in the dry?" (Luke xxiii, 31.)

Following the example of the saints, let us live in continual remembrance of our sins, being the more careful not to forget them, that God has pardoned them with greater mercy. Be convinced that the surest sign of this pardon which we have obtained will be found in that compunction of heart which we should constantly experience within us. Beware of the levity which nowadays appears in so many who seem to think no more of their sins after absolution; as if it were not written that sin, although forgiven, should never cease to inspire the sinful soul with true fear. Indeed, it cannot be said of such persons that love has dispelled their fear; for this is evident: either they have no love at all, or very little.

You will find another most powerful motive for fostering the salutary fear of the Lord by considering our entire dependence on divine grace and the terrible danger to which we are exposed by its abuse. Grace is given to all, but it does not fructify in all, because it is in the power of man to obstruct and hinder its operations. Now this divine and merciful grace is come down upon you. It has converted you and placed you on the most perfect and the surest way to salvation. As sanctifying grace, it may be suddenly withdrawn, in consequence of mortal sin, and leave the soul in utter death and ruin; as actual grace, it may, in consequence of an affection for venial sin and frequent resistance on the part of the soul, become rare, weak and barely sufficient. In fact, a soul, accustomed to more powerful assistance, if surrounded by snares and enemies, will surely succumb, sooner or later, and will then have no cause for murmuring against God, Who owes nothing to the creature, and sees that inestimable succour which He has unremittingly bestowed, despised and rejected.

The fear of the Lord, therefore, is a well-founded sentiment and the support of the entire edifice of perfection. It must be extremely necessary even to a soul in the more advanced stages of the spiritual life, since we see it roused by God with the greatest energy in such a one as the seraphic St. Theresa, after the ecstacies which were the reward of her love.

Let us take every precaution against be coming insensible to the motives of the fear of the Lord, a symptom of one of the most dangerous maladies of the soul. In such a state, the heart of man is both hardened and impervious; the best means to soften, subdue and strengthen it is the supernatural fear of the Lord. Experience teaches that conversions resulting from mere sentiment are not lasting, unless this blessed fear, in some way or other, come to shield man against inconstancy, indifference and pride.

Imitating the example of the holy Fathers of the desert who retired into solitude, in order to meditate on and to prepare themselves for the judgment of God, make the truths of this chapter the frequent subject of your meditations and you will soon learn the value of this fear of the Lord. And beholding you sincerely humbled at the thought of His dreadful judgment, He shall sweetly transform this first sentiment so that from the fear of arousing His wrath, because He is terrible, you will advance to the fear of offending Him, because He is good. Most seriously and firmly resolved to walk the way of purgation, you shall be called to mount still higher, to follow the straight pathway with a confidence the surer, that it has risen in a soul profoundly stirred and made conscious of the only true reality by the most lawful, formidable and reasonable fear that can agitate man here below.

Humility should, henceforth, strike deep roots in the soul. For no other virtue prepares it so well for the true love of God and union with Him. At whatever degree of charity you may arrive, take care occasionally to reanimate your courage and perseverance by the contemplation of the dreadful judgments of God.

By applying the maxims of this chapter, we shall become staunch Christians, thus laying the one foundation of religious life which is not open to delusion and danger.

CHAPTER V

ON FAITH

The fear of the Lord, so necessary to every Christian, docility to His teachings, the study of His precepts, abhorrence for all that He condemns, all these assume the virtue of faith, which alone reveals to us Jesus Christ, His rights over us and what we have to fear if we do not listen to His voice.

Faith is the beginning of our salvation: by it we come into contact with God; without it, we should remain in darkness; if our faith is lively, we are full of light; if it is weak, then our entire soul becomes languid. Therefore the Apostle says: "Without faith, it is impossible to please God." (Heb. xi, 6.)

Now, the faithful in the world can maintain their relations with God only by means of this virtue, which places before them the sublime motives which must regulate their lives. How, then, can the religious preserve the life of his soul and advance on the more perfect way which he must constantly pursue, unless he possess a lively faith? Hence our great duty of acquiring this virtue in an eminent degree and making a steady progress in it. In order to accomplish this, turn to God, and ask Him for an increase of this admirable gift, beseeching Him with the Apostles: "Domine, adauge nobis fidem." (Luke xvii, 5.) Aspire constantly after the supernatural, and learn to appreciate and to judge all things from the standpoint of faith alone. It is that of God Himself, who mercifully sent into our midst His purest light to prevent our minds from going astray and our corrupt nature from failing into error.

The state to which you aspire is foolishness in the eyes of the world. Experience will show, that it is possible to succeed in it only if, with singleness of purpose, you model your thoughts, impressions, even your inclinations, after the life and actions of our Lord, which have nothing in common with what is purely natural, after the holy Rule, which involves conditions altogether contrary to those induced by our natural propensities and finally, after the example of the Saints, who victoriously put nature under foot because, being foolish in the eyes of the world, they were filled with the wisdom of God.

Strive constantly to effect this union in thought and intention with Jesus Christ and His saints. Establish yourselves firmly in faith and the safety of your entire spiritual edifice will be assured. Experience will make it evident to you that your perseverance will be certain so long as this foundation remains unshaken, but that as soon as it threatens to collapse, you, like the Christian in the world, will be unable to retain your foothold on that height to which you were guided by faith and where faith alone can uphold you. The prophet tells us, "The just shall live in his faith." (Hab. ii, 4.) If this be true of the simple Christian, how much more of the religious! Faith must be his element, his nourishment, his joy, his delight; for it is first and principally through faith that God communicates Himself to man and transforms and supernaturalizes his life.

The eyes of those faithful to grace are opened by this divine light, and all things appear in a purer and fuller aspect. The world and this present life are transformed in their sight. They clearly behold the immensity of God and the nothingness of the creature. The goodness of God, the honour and happiness attained in denying one's self for his sake, the insignificance of the sacrifices involved in following Him are then unfolded and fill them with joy and peace. All these blessings we owe to faith. Its holy enthusiasm should be ever active in us and should be constantly renewed by giving thanks to God, who has condescended to enlighten us, and also by earnest prayer for the increase in us of this ineffable gift.

Let the spirit of faith breathe forth in all your words and actions. You should be most responsive to everything that promotes it, but should shrink from that which is contrary to, or hinders it. From it arises a supreme reverence for whatever has reference to God and a tender veneration of holy things, even the least of them. Those objects should be particularly dear to you which are sanctified by the prayers of the Church and bear direct or indirect reference to the supernatural. Living in this blessed atmosphere which the spirit of faith diffuses around the faithful soul, you will be safe against numberless dangers and discern more distinctly the voice of God within you. Another effect of this state, which should be common to all Christians, is the perceptible diminution of the power exercised over the soul by Satan, who generally opens his attacks by awakening the spirit of rationalism, which is, however, neutralized instantly by faith.

Let it be understood that the faith so necessary for us does not consist in that purely intellectual conviction of the truth of Christianity which may also be obtained from study and observation. Most assuredly, reason must be employed to the degree granted by God for gaining an unshaken conviction of the fact of divine revelation and the reality of the mysteries by means of which God condescends to come into relation with man. It may, however, be easily noticed, from practical life, that this faith is not sufficient for the sanctification of man. The evil spirits and the damned in hell have this faith and are neither saved nor converted by it. It is the virtue of faith, and not the more or less learned deduction of the arguments of the teachers, that saves and converts. The Christian believes, because he wills to believe; because he is humble before God; because he knows that God will impart His light to the simple of heart; and that the faith of reason remains sterile as long as it is not supplemented by the faith of the heart.

To aspire to this virtue of faith must, therefore, be the first concern of the religious. He should, so to say, possess it in a higher degree than that necessary for the simple faithful, since he is called to a closer union with God, who dwells in an inaccessible light, in the midst of which we must, to avoid being blinded, close our mortal eyes in love and confidence.

From this it follows that the religious should profess unbounded adherence to holy Church, which has been intrusted by her Divine Spouse with the special charge of leading us to this light. Let us not be content with submitting our reason to the formal decisions of her whom the Apostle calls "the pillar and ground of truth." (Tim. iii. 15) Let our hearts also incline towards the pious beliefs which she favours, and be filled with horror by everything that deviates from her holy teachings, assured that we shall be in the right as long as we remain united with her in even the least point of doctrine. Let us inquire into the different ways by which the spirit of God worketh in her and resolve to conform heart and soul to the slightest manifestation of her views and desires. And since the centre of truth and life in the holy Church is the Apostolic See, we will profess a tender devotedness to all the prerogatives of the Roman Pontiff: to his infallibility in doctrine, to his full and divine authority over the entire Church, which is greater than the authority of any other power on earth, even the Oecumenical Council, because he is the true Vicar of Christ. Let us beware of the contrary teaching, which is incompatible with true science, as well as with the spirit of faith. * If anyone be unable to divest himself of the prejudices which he may have imbibed on this point in the world, he should withdraw rather than injure himself and others by remaining in a society whose first law is adherence to the Roman doctrine, concerning the divinely established monarchy of the Church.

Finding us united to His Spouse by the bond of sincere submission, the Divine Saviour will diffuse in us this spirit of faith which will become a reservoir of all graces, the principle of a supernatural enlightenment that shall guide and confirm us in all things and prepare us to behold, for all eternity, in unveiled splendour, that indescribable light whose faintest ray we shall have prized so dearly even in this world.

* These pages were written by the author long before the Vatican Council. Dom Guéranger, in reviving the Benedictine Order in France, demanded, as we see, an explicit Profession of belief in the infallibility of the Supreme Pontiff as a necessary condition of admittance into the novitiate.

CHAPTER VI

ON HOPE

The consideration of the infinite blessings promised by faith should excite in us the desire for the Supreme Good which it points out to us, and the beauty of that virtue should win our hearts to seek it by every means available.

Faith is a light destined not only to shine before us, but it should likewise guide our footsteps and lead us to another virtue essential to the Christian, and still more so to the monk, namely, the virtue of hope. Without this virtue, the Christian does not exist and the religious is inconceivable. But he whose soul abounds in hope can truly be said to be on the way which leads to his last end.

Hope is the firm and supernatural trust in God, that He will graciously assist us to arrive at a happy eternity, provided we profit by His grace and, furthermore, that He will always grant us His grace in proportion to our needs, provided we ask for it in humility.

Strive to comprehend that the bounty of God towards His creatures being infinite and proclaimed by the works of His most sublime mercy, He demands this confidence in Him, by which we render Him justice. The efficacy of this sentiment is such that the Apostle does not hesitate to assert that the Christian "is already saved by hope." (Rom. viii, 24.) Now, as the simple faithful is supported in the service of God by the firm confidence that the Lord will endow him with the necessary grace and strength, so also the religious, for stronger reasons, will persevere on his higher way, with more or less facility, according to the influence which this virtue exercises over him.

It is, consequently, necessary that the novice apply himself to its practice with heroic zeal. Hope is a virtue only in as far as its existence exacts of us defence against two enemies which continually menace it and which we must fight with undaunted fortitude.

The first is want of confidence, which makes us fearful in regard to receiving the grace necessary for performing all our duties as Christians and religious.

It is from this side that the devil assaults sometimes the best and most supernatural vocations. With affectation, and often with exaggeration, he vividly depicts to us the sacrifices which we must make until death, if we wish to arrive at the perfection expected of us by God.

He reminds us of our weakness, of our past infidelities, of the scanty energy that is in us. Taking at the same time the greatest care to hide from our eyes the most powerful goodness and liberality of God towards the soul which consents to hope in Him, this evil spirit succeeds in undermining our firmest resolutions and thus places us on the verge of perdition. By means of this treacherous scheme, he has destroyed the welfare of an immense number of Christian souls and seduced from their vocation many souls called to the religious life.

When you perceive the hissing of this old serpent, be sure to stop up your ears, because this distrust which he wishes to sow in you is an infamous blasphemy against the infinite bounty of God. Consider, that though nothing may seem more true than the repugnance of nature to embrace what is good and above all, what is better, nothing more real than our natural weakness and laxity, yet there is something still more certain, namely, the promise of God concerning grace, which is always more powerful than nature, something more real, namely, the uninterrupted bestowal of grace, the constancy with which this grace is put at our disposal and the means by which we may ever increase it, if we only ask for it with humility and perseverance.

Reanimated by this thought, which faith in the word of God suggests in us, let us bless the Lord, because by teaching us that despair is the only sin which cannot be forgiven, He has revealed to us that hope has the gift of moving Him and can open to the soul the way of reconciliation with its Creator. Never allow yourselves to be intimidated in exercising this cardinal virtue, which the Apostle compares with the anchor of safety that protects the ship against the raging billows. May you, for the rest of your life, hold fast to the saying of our holy Patriarch that the novice should "never lose hope in the mercy of God; de Dei misericordia nunquam desperare."" (Ch. 4. 73.)

There is yet another rock, not less threatening to the virtue of hope, if not carefully shunned. This rock on which many have already suffered shipwreck is presumption.

Distrust injures God in His bounty, presumption attacks his honour. It seems to tell Him that man has no need of grace, or that he has such a right to this divine help that he need not disquiet himself about it. Such a disposition is fraught with the greatest danger to one's vocation and even to his eternal salvation.

You would run the risk of being ensnared by it, to the greatest detriment of your soul, should you cease to feel your entire dependence on divine grace, not only in order to advance, but even in order to maintain your position; not only for that which pertains to the permanent condition of the soul, but for every action in particular. You would not only make no progress, but a relapse would be inevitable. Consider often the abyss of our unworthiness and the immense bounty of God, who has the right to impart His treasures to humble souls only who unceasingly appeal to him, and may refuse them daily to those wretched souls who are so sadly blindfolded by presumption. Now, he who abandons humiliation and does not ask for grace with fervour, is very apt to fall into this dangerous vice. Hence, watch carefully that you be not lulled into a false confidence, which, sooner or later, would most cruelly deceive you.

Assured, on the one hand, of the all-powerful goodness of God who glories in saving and sanctifying His creatures and leading them to eternal bliss, and convinced, on the other hand, that humble and confident prayer obtains all things from the heavenly Munificence, you will feel the blessings of hope so much the more, the less you esteem yourselves before God. This virtue will procure for you a joyful heart, interior sweetness, a most profound tranquillity, the anticipation of possessing the infinite happiness which awaits you and, lastly, the necessary courage to conquer self in all things, and, enlightened by faith, you will approach nearer to God, whom you are called to possess by love.

CHAPTER VII

ON THE LOVE OF GOD

Our Lord was not content with making His eternal truth shine forth to our view; He, at the same time, encouraged us to hope for the good things revealed by faith and deigned to call upon us to unite ourselves to Him by love. "The end of the law is charity," says the Apostle. (I Tim. i, 5.) And fearing lest we should deem this mutual love between God and man a fanciful idea altogether above our nature, He even commanded us to love Him, under pain of being eternally cast out from His presence. "Thou shalt love the Lord, thy God, with thy whole heart, and with thy whole soul, and with all thy strength" (Luke x, 97); and our Lord teaches us that this is the greatest and first commandment.

Considering the grandeur and undeniable urgency of this precept, the novice should henceforth look up to his state as that most suited for fulfilling it and bless God for the mercy accorded him in granting him the grace of a religious vocation.

Love of God constitutes the whole of Christian life. The other moral and theological virtues only prepare us for, and lead us to, the love of God. St. Augustine says: "Love and do what you will." He who truly loves God is safe against sin, because sin is the very contrary of love. To love God is the easiest and sweetest of all the commandments, though it is just the one which is violated most frequently and imperceptibly. Love of God brings us into the possession of God Himself. It is by love that heaven is heaven. It is the prime necessity of our being, because we can be happy only in loving the good, and this is God. This love is a holy debt, because God loved us first, continually works in us by His love and awaits with generous patience the return of the love we owe Him.

The obstacle which the love of God meets in man arises from various causes that arrest the creature in its flight and turn it from its last end, outside of which there is nothing but reprobation, for whoever will not love God in this world, shall be sentenced to hate Him for all eternity in hell. These causes are: Illusions, which cause us to forget the invitation extended us by God to love Him; the world, its maxims and example; attachment to material goods, to creatures and to self; lastly, want of support and encouragement. Let the novice gratefully acknowledge that the religious state removes all these barriers, and that for him who wishes to profit by the means it offers, the accomplishment of the greatest and first of the commandments is made easy.

The religious state establishes man in recollection and peace, as on a mountain whose summit reaches far into the sky. It produces in the soul that interior and exterior silence in which the word of God works freely, dissipates illusions and protects the soul against the unperceived insinuation of forgetfulness. By separating the religious from contact with the world, it also frees him from the dangers which this deceitful enemy presents in its maxims and example, avoided only with difficulty by him who lives in its midst. The attachment to material goods, to creatures and self being successfully fought by the exact observance of the holy vows, the soul finds again its primitive liberty, and tends with ease towards its divine centre. Such a soul, supported in every possible way by the Rule and the observances, which are a source of countless graces, strengthened by the example of others, called to order by exhortations and, if necessary, by reproofs and corrections, could be induced to desert the path of love only by obstinate and repeated resistance of good. This is happily of rare occurrence.

We must justly conclude from this that the religious has a greater assurance of his perseverance in the practice of this great commandment than anyone in the world. If only on this account, he should consider himself the happiest of men.

Let us firmly resolve to take advantage of the many graces lavished on us in order to advance in the love of God by concentrating all our powers to this blessed end. It is above all of greatest importance to know that this precept requires of us no laborious exertions. For the Lord Himself says to His chosen people: "This commandment that I command thee this day is not above thee, nor far off from thee, nor is it in heaven that thou shouldst say: Which of us can go up to heaven to bring it to us, and we may hear and fulfil it in work? Nor is it beyond the sea: that thou mayest excuse thyself and say: Which of us can cross the sea, and bring it unto us: that we may hear and do that which is commanded? But the word is very nigh unto thee, in thy mouth and in thy heart, that thou mayest do it." (Deut. xxx, 11—14.) To love God, we need then only follow the impulse of our hearts. The mere thought of His supreme amiability and the remembrance of his benefits suffice to maintain us in this charity which unites us with Him.

In the first place, be ever intent upon multiplying these treasures of eternal life. Make, as often as possible, explicit acts of love towards God. These acts, arising from an impulse of grace, have great power to enrich the source from which they emanate. In all the motives of your thoughts and actions, seek to give preference to the love of God. You will find it an excellent help, and your thoughts and actions will at the same time be raised to greater merit and higher dignity. Be habitually determined by the consideration of the love we owe to God in the sacrifices which you will have to make. For, if real, it will urge you to sacrifice and not to repose.

Whereas God prescribes to man several distinct moral and theological virtues, do not dispense yourselves from any one of them under the pretext that the love of God should be enough for you, but strive to unite this motive of love with those peculiar to the other virtues, by making them participate in the nature of divine love. Lastly, when you fail, look on your faults as infidelities to the love of God. This will greatly enable you to hasten the pardon which will be readily granted by the merciful Judge.

You should be eager to carry to the utmost perfection the motives of your love of God. Rest not content with a purely se1f-interested love which aims at personal welfare only. Consider, without ever ceasing to love God as your last end with this love of desire which springs from the virtue of love as its pure and holy source, without checking in its course the love of gratitude which should fill you with ever increasing acknowledgement of the blessings received from God, that there exists in Him an inexhaustible loveliness which justly excites our love apart from our own interests. You should endeavor to ascend, as far as human weakness permits, to this love for His sake, which effaces sin by remitting guilt and the punishment due, and which can unite, even in this world, the soul with its Creator.

Elicit to this end, according to the impulses of grace, acts of the love of benevolence, compliance and compassion, by which the soul embraces the interests of God with an ardour that is not dimmed by self-interest. Penetrate into the sense of the Lord's Prayer, the first three petitions of which convey to everyone who is able to comprehend them the expression of this love. In one word, let us act in all things with the conviction that as men, Christians and religious, we have a lofty and all-embracing duty to fulfil in this world, namely, the duty of loving God before all things and continually, with a love proportionate to the graces bestowed on us for the purpose of loving Him.

CHAPTER VIII

ON THE LOVE OF OUR LORD JESUS CHRIST

Such is the infinite bounty and love of God towards us that we have seen Him debase Himself to the condition of man and fill up, so to say, the chasm that separated us from Him, in order to obtain more effectively the return which is His just due. "In this we have known the charity of God, because He hath laid down His life for us." (I John iii, 6); and the Son of God says, even in the Old Testament, when describing the motive of His future coming in the flesh: "My delight is to be with the children of men." (Prov, viii, 31.) These advances which God has vouchsafed to make towards us should be appreciated by all with reverent astonishment. Considering that by the divine incarnation He made Himself flesh of our flesh, we shall understand how greatly this facilitated the great commandment of loving God. Let us often thank the Divine Goodness for thinking us worthy of being born after the accomplishment of the mystery of the Word made flesh, which broadened the way to Union with God in love. Jesus Christ is man as we are: he who loves Jesus Christ is already in the possession of the love of God, because Jesus Christ is God.

And how is it possible for man not to love this incarnate God? The Son of God presents Himself in this state with such infinite attractions that not to love Him man must either renounce his nature or acknowledge himself to be a degraded being. In fact, two reasons impel us to love our fellows: their charms of person and the benefits they bestow on us. Now, is it possible, in reading and meditating upon the holy Gospels, to resist the divine charm which pervades the words and actions of our Lord? When we behold Him in His infancy, what is more alluring than our Lord in the manger or in the loving arms of His most pure Mother? When we follow Him in the vigour of manhood, what is more affecting than His goodness, His compassion for the miseries of mankind, His patience, His condescension and the gentleness of His manner, that so sweetly tempers the gravity of His person as to gather about Him even the little children? What is more captivating than His teaching, in which the authority of a God lies hid beneath the most simple language, and overpowering and sublime truths penetrate the heart of the listener, flooding his mind with most vivid light? What is more touching than His predilection for sinners, those unfortunate sick, whose compassionate physician He is, those lost sheep for whom He is the unwearied shepherd? Lastly, what is more moving than the calmness with which He faces the death He foreknew, never protesting against the ingratitude of His enemies?

It is impossible that an upright man should meditate on this life—and the novices ought incessantly to study it—and not be moved and quickly captivated by the love of Him Who led this life on earth. If one may be moved at perceiving in another one of those traits which reveal a noble sentiment, and moved to such a degree as to feel his heart drawn towards this man whom he will never see, who has, perhaps, ceased centuries ago to dwell upon this earth, how is it possible to fortify one's heart against love towards Jesus, in Whom all is perfect, all complete, all inspired by the most generous love for us.

Now, it is God Himself, whom we love in loving Jesus Christ. Thus the great commandment of charity has come nigh to us, as if to lay a snare, and we have fallen into it: he who loves the Son of Mary, loves the Son of God; and he who loves the Son of God, loves the Father and the Holy Ghost, because these three are one in the same substance.

But when, without turning our eyes from the ineffable charms of our celestial Lover, we come to consider His benefits, is it possible that this love may not triumph over our cold hearts? We were His enemies: He died for us the death of the cross; we were lost for all eternity: He has saved us by delivering Himself up for us; we have crucified Him by our sins: He set forth His glory in our pardon. The slightest reparation offered by Him would have sufficed superabundantly to compensate for the outrage committed by a thousand worlds against the divine Majesty, but to insure our devotion to Him, He has willed to shed amidst awful torments, all His blood, even to the last drop. His sacrifice, offered up for the whole human race, was made in particular for every one of us, as if every one of us had been the only person culpable and the only object of His coming into this world.

Is it not evident that he who thus mentally rehearses the motives of loving our Saviour would be the most degraded of men and would not deserve to live, if he did not feel himself pierced by that love? And is it not also true that he whose heart is not totally corrupted by self-love, nor wholly pressed down by the disgraceful weight of sensuality cannot think of the benefits of the God-man without feeling himself drawn to the hove of such a benefactor, a love superior to self-love?

Let us, then, say once more, the great commandment is accomplished: the mmiyst cries of the Incarnate Word have been the (liv time bait which has allured us. Following the natural bent of our hearts which inclines us to love our fellow-men for their attractions and for the benefits they bestow, we have risen, through Jesus Christ, the God man, to the love of the invisible God, who has created us to love and serve Him.

It is not hard to grasp the blessed facilities which our Lord has, in this way, extended to us for the accomplishment of this fundamental precept of the Christian and religious life. You will perceive that everything depends on the firmness and constancy of this love towards our Lord Jesus Christ. Therefore, let us often say with the Apostle: "Who shall separate us from the love of Jesus Christ?" (Rom. viii, 35.) And that this charity be fortified and increased in your soul, neglect nothing which may preserve the impress on made by the perfections and benefits of the incarnate Son of God. Let them become the most familiar subject of your thoughts and affections. For this very same purpose, strive daily to advance in the understanding of the Gospels, which will then indeed be good tidings to you. For, in them you will learn the art of loving God by loving the Divine Saviour, who has bestowed on us such marvellous favours.

CHAPTER IX

ON PERFECTION

God, by revealing himself to man by faith, arousing his hope in an eternal reunion with the supreme Good and commanding him to love His Creator and Redeemer, proposed to Himself an end which relates first of all to man's state in this world. This end is that man here below should aspire to perfection.

Perfection is the greatest possible harmony of relation between the creature and its God. It is the result of the conformity of the creature to the holiness of God by exemption from sin and the acquisition of the virtues, of which charity is the most lofty and the most extended in its influence upon the others.

From this it follows that the Christian has a real obligation to strive after perfection, and must exercise himself in it according to the amount of grace which he receives. Otherwise it could be truly said that God either did not care to see the plan which He conceived realized by His creature, or that the latter could justly refuse to accomplish the purpose for which He wrested man from perdition and ransomed him from hell. Nothing could be more odious, nothing more foolish, than such perverse ideas as these. And that the Christian may not allow himself to he duped with respect to this precept of perfection, which comprises all others, our Lord has said: "Be you therefore perfect as also your heavenly Father is perfect." (Matt. v, 48.) By these words, He shows us the model upon which we are to mould not only our actions, but also our thoughts and aspirations.

Imbued with this doctrine, let the novices examine their past life, and they will observe that they have never committed sin without losing sight, at least momentarily, of the duty of striving after perfection. The very thought of this duty would have sufficed to preserve them from falling into sin. You can easily notice that your hope of persevering in the state of sanctifying grace is steadfast only as long as you pursue the object of perfection. You would endanger cv elm your eternal welfare by neglecting this object or allowing it to vanish from your sight. The sanctity of our heavenly Father shall, therefore, be the aim of our efforts. Created and regenerated according to the likeness of God, it is our first duty to acquire this similarity in so far as we are able until we shall be reunited with Him forever in that habitation where as the Apostle says, "we shall be like to Him." (I John, iii, 2.)

However, do not become discouraged, if, in spite of your resolute struggles, you should still find yourselves so far removed from your model by reason of sins not yet sufficiently expiated or faults frequently committed, or on account of the infinite end pro posed. Derive great consolation from the thought that the perfection acquired is not of this world; the greatest Saints have re alized it to its fullest extent only in heaven. It is time continual desire for perfection that made them Saints, a desire and tendency never weakened in them by their faults amid

imperfections.

Have this great Christian obligation always firmly fixed before your eyes and pay no heed to the objections of self-love, which would distinguish between the rights of God and our own ill-understood interests. When you consider how seriously imperiled is the welfare of him who renounces his efforts towards perfection, how such a one alienates himself from the love of God, it will always be easy for you, with the never-failing help of grace, to remain fixed in this firm resolution, which will be your security as well as the consolation of your life.

The arch enemy of mankind never tires in his attempts to stifle the desire after perfection, frightening man by the inmost absurd illusions. According to him, the path of perfection offers nothing but thorns. Despise these hallucinations and you will gradually comprehend more and more clearly that nothing is more just and wise in a Christian than the abhorrence of sin and its occasions and the longing after every virtue. Thus you shall come nearer to God, who is infinitely holy and has destined us to be united with Him for all eternity. Consider what constitutes perfection. It does not consist in this or that extraordinary act of which we read in the lives of the Saints and which might seem to us above our abilities. It is not through such acts that they became Saints, but by the constant desire for perfection, their acts being the outgrowth of this desire and its expression, more or less varied, according to the nature of the graces they possessed.

We have just reasons to be especially thankful to God, as He has vouchsafed to summon us to the religious state which forms, in the holy Church, the school of perfection. In fact, the religious life is founded upon the practice of the evangelical counsels, and these aim at the removal of the numerous barriers which retard the Christian on the path of perfection. He who concludes that it is better to devote himself to God by holy poverty, chastity and obedience and faithfully abides by his contract, will certainly reach the perfection that assures him union with God. This perfection shall be his repose, his recompense even here below, and he will bear testimony to the word of our Lord which says: "My yoke is sweet and my burden light." (Matt. xi, 30.) The obstacles to every resolution of seeking perfection, which are awakened by the love of self and exterior objects, are put to flight by the voluntary and constant practice of the divine counsels. The love of God, which is called by the Apostle "the bond of perfection" (Col. iii, 14), will then reign supreme in the soul and become, without difficulty, the governing principle of our entire life.

Lastly, remember the call to perfection, extended to Christians, and the heroic struggles which those must undergo who practise it in the midst of the world. Do not forget, that you have been marked with a special predilection in being placed, by your holy vocation, on a road where the light that illumines the soul never grows dim and where innumerable graces that support and correct are hourly lavished on you, so that, to miss the goal, not only incurable weakness would be necessary, but also obstinate resistance, from which may the bounty of God ever preserve His own!

CHAPTER X

ON THE IMITATION OF OUR LORD JESUS CHRIST

Just as, in order to make sure in us the fulfilment of the great and indispensable precept of charity, God has deigned by making himself man, to bring near to us the object of the love which is essential, so also He has seen fit, in this same mystery of the Divine Incarnation, to set quite within our reach the type of the perfection to which He obliges us to aspire.

By becoming man, God, in His infinite goodness, brought near to us the essential object of our love, to insure our accomplishment of the great and indispensable precept of charity. With the same end in view, I he has also thought it proper to send the model for that perfection to which He obliges us altogether within our reach, by the mystery of the Divine incarnation. The imitation of our heavenly Father would have been very difficult for feeble and ignorant creatures as we are, but the Son of God, perfect as the Father, assumed our nature and, coming down to this earth, acted, spoke and willed as a man-God could act, speak or will and thenceforward we had only to imitate Him, in order to arrive at the imitation of God. Therefore the Apostle teaches us that "whom the Father foreknew, He also predestinated to be made conformable to the image of His Son." (Rom. xiii, 29.)

We ought, then, to render unceasing thanks to the Divine Mercy for having ordained us to be born after the Incarnation of the Divine Word; for the lustre of His example enlightens and guides us, as His precious blood has ransomed us. The primitive man, created in justice and holiness, exists no more.

Sin has made of him a ruin, in which the divine image is no longer discernible. Therefore, Jesus Christ was given to us, not only as Redeemer, but also as model. In him we can see what we should become in order to resemble God once more. St. John tells us, in one of his Epistles, that our greatest hope on the day of judgment will be in this, that "as He is, we also are in this world."

(S. John, iv, 17.) The same Apostle says in another place: "He that saith he abideth in Him, ought himself also to walk even as He walked." (I John, ii, 6.) St. Paul explains this in one word, when he admonishes the faithful: "Put ye on our Lord Jesus Christ." (Rom. xiii, 14.)

In gratitude to the ineffable goodness of God, which decreed to bring down from heaven the type following which we should be remodelled and become perfect as our heavenly Father, we should have nothing more at heart than the most thorough study of this divine and human ideal, which shall suddenly confront us on the day of judgment. Our Divine Saviour, speaking to His heavenly Father, expresses Himself also thus: "Now this is eternal life: that they may know Thee, the only true God, and Jesus Christ whom Thou hast sent." (St. John xvii, 3.) Every Christian should infer from these words that to know Jesus Christ is his greatest concern in this world, because it leads to eternal life.

Let the novices, accordingly, comprehend that the study of our Lord by reading the holy Gospels supplies the surest means for nourishing and developing this love of their Redeemer, just as attention to all that He did, all that He said and all that He was, as related in the sacred text, will be the source of that imitation which leads to the perfection required by God. As an incentive to this research, which is to result in eternal happiness, often refresh in your memory what St. Luke teaches us of the Blessed Virgin: that she contemplated the actions of our Lord, had them constantly present in her thoughts, and "kept all these words, pondering them in her heart." (ii, 19.) By this constant and most loving study, Mary succeeded in realizing the model of her Divine Son and rose to perfection. Every disciple of Jesus Christ ought to do likewise according to his ability.

You should consider it a great honour to have been withdrawn from the world and its vain tumult, in order to study thoroughly our Lord and to devote yourselves to His imitation. This should be your constant thought and effort, because if this imitation be realized, everything may be counted for you as gained, but all will be lost, if unfortunately it should be wanting to you. A Father of time Church (Tertullian) said, and he did not say too much: "Christianus alter Christus." In fact, what is meant by a Christian? A member of Jesus Christ. Now, the members have the same life and inner feeling as the head.

This imitation of the man-God, this incorporation with Jesus Christ, is undoubtedly a hard task, and costs nature many a sacrifice. But even so, let us bear in mind that there is no choice. We must resemble either the man of the earth or the man of heaven. If we preserve the features of the earthly man, we shall be damned and thrust into hell-fire; if, on the other hand, the heavenly

Father recognize in us the features of His Son, who is the heavenly man, He will reclaim us as His children, and where Jesus is, we also shall be.

It is true, we cannot resolve to imitate Jesus Christ, if we do not love Him. But have we not seen that this is our first duty, the strictest justice and our dearest consolation in this vale of tears? Therefore, be determined to remain faithful in this love, and generously acknowledge that nothing is more just than that we become like to Him who has taken our likeness upon Him out of love for us. Moreover, you have no right to find that reform severe which makes us like to God, by purifying our life from the bad germs which would have caused our eternal ruin.

In conclusion, remember that this reform in man, wrought after the model of Jesus Christ, is in no wise the work of nature, but the work of grace. This is never refused to us and can be increased by prayer in the SpOuse to which God always grants what is conducive to the progress of the soul. May you, therefore, incessantly pray that Jesus Christ be accomplished in you; that His life find its expression in your lives and animate your whole being. Be heartily and loyally attached to this great end of our life, returning to it again and again, and taking advantage of every opportunity to attain it. When studying the lives of the most Blessed Virgin and the Saints, search out the cause of their holiness. Seeing that it is nothing else than their conformity to the deeds and sentiments of Jesus Christ, let it ever become clearer to you what God expects of you, and apply to yourselves in humility and gratitude the word addressed by Christ to every one of us in the person of St. Peter: "Come, follow me: veni, sequere me." (John xxi, 19.)

CHAPTER XI

ON THE EVANGELICAL COUNSELS

The imitation of our Lord Jesus Christ being the obligatory way for everyone who wishes to arrive at eternal salvation and glory, the supreme wisdom of God has ordained that the imitation of a type so elevated should be realized to different degrees. Taking into consideration human frailty, and resolved to dispense His grace most justly according to the measure of His good pleasure, our Saviour gave to man precepts and counsels. The precepts, obligatory on all men, represent the essential conditions without which there is no salvation. The Counsels refer to those who are called to ascend still higher in the imitation of our Lord, who realized, in this life, the matter of the counsels in admirable perfection and plenitude.

Our notion of the evangelical counsels cannot be too lofty; be it that we behold their type in our Lord, or that we consider them by all men on earth, would not have sufficed to reproduce the features of the Incarnate Son of God. This, then, is the reason why the Divine Restorer of the primitive man vouchsafed to employ the inducement of a reward, promising a hundredfold to those who keep His counsels in order to allure thereby the greatest number of those who were bought by His precious blood.

You should, consequently, show most sincere acquiescence in the merciful intentions of our Redeemer. Render Him humble thanks, because, by calling you to the religious state, which is the school or the evangelical counsels, He has placed you on His privileged way, where the glory of God is sought with the greatest solicitude by the most perfect imitation of his Son. Cease not from asking Him for the grace not to fall back from this superior degree, where you have been gratuitously established by grace, and be humbled at the consideration that it did not enter into the designs of God to call all men to this same favour.

Often call to mind the calling of the Apostles, who were the first ones chosen to leave all things that they might devote themselves not only to the p1(~(e1)tK of our Lord, but also in their relation to salvation. From the first point of view, these divine counsels merit our esteem on account of the union which they establish between our Lord and the one who practises them. As to the second point of view, our idea of their importance cannot be too high, since the practice of the counsels insures that of the precepts and is consequently the most sure highway to salvation. And this last truth is so evident that very often, even in the midst of the world, the practice of the Christian life would be impossible of realization without rising, in certain instances, to the observance of the counsels.

In giving the divine counsels, our Lord could have no other intention than to see them followed. If He did not make them obligatory on all men, He at least desired their accomplishment in a certain number of This faithful. His wisdom and honour are likewise involved in it, as also the realization of the Gospel of which not a single iota is to remain unfulfilled. To find grace, it was necessary that the earth constantly reflect, in the sight of God, the image of His Son, realized in humanity. Now, the simple precepts, though observed to the very letter to His counsels. Their recompense consisted, at first, in familiar intercourse with their Divine Redeemer, in initiation into His secrets and in the sharing of His mission; at the end of time, they shall be seen sitting on thrones, judging the twelve tribes of Israel. A similar lot is reserved for those who imitate them: intimacy with Jesus Christ, who has no secrets from them, and the highest distinctions in the eternal kingdom.

Turning then his eyes upon his own frailty, which he knows from experience, the novice should acknowledge how much he owes to the Divine Mercy which, desirous of assuring his salvation, has set him on a way that is most likely to lead him to this the one thing necessary. The practice of the counsels, so greatly facilitated in the religious state, insures him the highest merits and guarantees the practice of the precepts. Thus he will, at the same time, arrive at salvation and perfection. For such is the efficacy of the religious vocation, when embraced by a man of good will, that it conducts him to the Supreme Good with much more ease than could be acquired in the world, where every thing is of the nature of an impediment, whilst in the religious state everything is a help.

He shall clearly understand that this religious vocation is a way graciously opened to a great number of souls, although only a few pursue it. Indeed, God calls them to the religious state sometimes by an interior affection for it, at other times by external circumstances. It is He who infuses this affection, and it is His grace that gives rise to the circumstances. He calls the just and the sinner; the just, to satiate his hunger and to still his thirst after justice; the sinner, to make him just and holy. Such wonders of grace are achieved by the practice of the evangelical counsels, which elevate our entire life and transform it in Jesus Christ.

Let us thus inform ourselves as to the nature of the religious vocation, which is so different from that to the holy Priesthood. The latter depends entirely on God, to whom alone it belongs to choose His ministers, that is to say, those whom He wishes to set up as mediators between Himself and man. The former, on the contrary, depends both on divine grace and on ourselves. Faith illumines us as to the advantages of the perfect life; grace urges us to embrace it and gives us the strength to practise it. Man follows or resists this attraction. We see that our Lord invites man to embrace the way of the counsels in the holy Gospel, but when the Priesthood is concerned He makes the choice Himself. There is, consequently, no power on earth, be it civil or even ecclesiastical, which has the right to prevent any one from following the way of the counsels, since no one has the right to prevent the just from drawing nearer to God, or the sinner from seizing the means which assures for him the amendment of his life and his progress in righteousness.

1. Religious Poverty.

The evangelical counsels may be summed up into three principal ones, the first of which is poverty, that is, the complete and unconditional renunciation of all earthly possessions, of whatsoever value they may be. Holy poverty is the first degree in the perfect imitation of our Lord. He was born in a borrowed stable; worked in the sweat of His brow, to gain His livelihood; lived upon alms during the years of His preaching; was nailed naked to the cross, and his body was finally laid in a tomb not his own. It was impossible to make us better understand that absolute poverty is a way of merit and of reparation. For, indeed, it quenches time desire for earthly goods, called by St. John the concupiscence of the eyes, which is one of the chief sources of offence towards God and the ruin of souls. Holy poverty is the beginning of the perfect life. Hence our Lord has said: "If thou wilt be perfect, go sell what thou hast, and give to the poor, and thou shalt have treasure in heaven." (Matt. xix, 21.) There is, then, no life in perfect harmony with that of Jesus Clirist, which is not effectually despoiled of earthly goods, and holy poverty must be our first step in order to enter upon this happy life.

Facts have repeatedly demonstrated that this virtue is the basis of the entire structure of the holy religious state. Moreover, everything may be expected of a religious family in whose bosom poverty is faithfully observed and held in honour. It may likewise be noted that, where the same is violated or neglected, there also the other fundamental principles of the religious life become shaken and soon fall together. In truth, a violation of religious poverty, no matter how trifling, is a perjury, because this virtue is the subject of a vow. Besides this, it is a veritable theft, because he who is guilty of it has no right over the thing which he assumes to be his. It is true that the matter is grave or light according to the value of the thing, but the perjury and theft are not less real.

It is, therefore, necessary that the religious who is desirous of persevering in the constant practice of poverty have a true love for this indispensable virtue. And how can he fail to love it, when he remembers the wonderful zeal with which our Lord Himself practised it; the rigour with which He enjoined its observance on His Apostles; the ardour with which it was promoted in the primitive Church of Jerusalem, all burning with the fire of the Holy Ghost?

Filled with respect for this fundamental virtue and eagerly longing after the treasure in heaven promised by our Lord, let the novice wish for the day when he may effectively practise this first of the counsels. Let him acquire an adequate idea of the nature and practice of this noble and holy virtue. You must understand that he who has taken the vow of poverty, ought not to have any desire for those things which he has left, nor to long after anything whatever. To be attached to objects given for his use, e.g., a book, furniture, his cell, etc., would be to fail in the poverty he has promised. The privations which may at times come upon the religious should be endured with cheerfulness, provided they are not prejudicial to his health, because then he will be a religious in the full sense of the word. For nothing is more contrary to the monastic spirit than that anxious solicitude with which one arranges all his affairs, so that nothing be wanting to him, whereby he seizes also upon things more comfortable than necessary. It is even wrong to aspire without permission to the private use of things which were not destined for such use. Finally, the religious is bound in conscience to make economical use of things regularly distributed for his personal needs, considering them as objects lent to him, of which he must take care with probity and delicacy of feeling.

Being also instructed as to the extent and the practice of holy poverty, the brethren of the novitiate will prepare themselves for it with a holy ??? yearning, happy to renounce already, in their desires, the goods and material advantages of this world in order to possess God. Be not troubled in the least by the events of our times, when the conspiracies of thie enemies of our faith are, in a special manner, directed against the revival of the religious state, but deem yourselves exceedingly honoured because it has pleased the Lord to count on you as He did on the Apostles, whom He summoned from their boats and nets, in order to send them into the world as lambs into the midst of wolves.

To show the sincerity with which you aspire to become the poor of Jesus Christ, commence, as soon as possible, to banish from your conversation all terms denoting property. Consequently, restrict, as much as possible, the use of things that belong to you, accustoming yourselves to be satisfied with what is strictly necessary. When you happen to lose, destroy, or injure anything belonging to the monastery, you will accuse yourselves in Chapter and do penance as the professed do. Should you perceive in yourselves any repugnance toward the privations imposed by religions poverty as to the food, the furnishings and the rest, rejoice and gladly harden yourselves in the sacrifice laid upon you by the renunciation of ease and property, calling to mind that this is what you sought at your entrance into the monastery.

In this way should the novice prepare himself for the taking of the vow of holy poverty and ripen in the spirit of his vocation. These supernatural sentiments are fostered by various means, as, meditation on the vanity of natural goods, from which man will be separated forever by death, the contemplation of the life of our Lord, who being rich, as the Apostle says, became poor for our sake and, lastly, the remembrance of the many kings and princes, queens and princesses who renounced wealth and crowns and whatever could flatter the senses or vanity, in order to become poor and detached from everything that is perishable, happy to resemble thereby our Saviour and proud to acquire by this means true riches, lasting honours and the eternal reward.

2. On Chastity.

The second of the evangelical counsels is chastity, to which our Lord directs our attention when He calls those blessed who have renounced the pleasures of sense "for the kingdom of heaven." (Matt. xix, 12.) St. Paul unfolds to us also its importance when he proposes perfect continency as that which is "better for man" (I Cor. vii, 38), because it sanctifies man in body and soul. But since chastity is a virtue imposed on all men, even outside of the religious state, — though it reaches its perfection only in this state — it is expedient forthwith to expose the whole Christian doctrine on this subject, that such an important matter may be fully comprehended.

The holy virtue of chastity seeks to control the sensual appetites by subjecting them to the law of the Spirit. It maintains man in his dignity and causes his soul continually to reflect the image of God who is a spirit. The vice opposed to chastity degrades man, reverses the economy of creation by giving predominance to the lower eleutient and stifling the soul under the pressure of the senses. Nothing could be more adverse to the decrees of the Creator. He, therefore, willed to join the obligation of continency to the exercise of the very rights he conceded to the conjugal state. It is in obedience to a fundamental principle of his existence that man should constantly strive to shake off the yoke of the senses. Not only every exterior act against holy purity is forbidden to him, but he is likewise bound to secure heart and soul against every willful desire or delight in respect to that which is forbidden by this virtue. Such is the delicacy of holy purity that the infringement of its obligations does not admit lightness of matter; want of sufficient consideration or imperfect consent may alone render venial a sin which would have been mortal otherwise.

From this it follows, that man should avail himself of every means to persevere in holy purity, because this virtue is indispensable for him. Now there are two obstacles which bring it about that this virtue can exist in us only by dint of warfare. In the first place, we are, in consequence of original sin, loaded with the weight of concupiscence, which destroys the equilibrium between the flesh and the spirit, and makes the former, weak as it is, the tyrant over the latter. In the second place, the holy virtue of chastity is an object of particular hatred to the devil, who is humiliated on seeing man ascend, through chastity, by the spirit; notwithstanding his human weakness. Wherefore this fallen angel is always ready to attack us from what he knows to be our weakest side.

Man, nevertheless, must not consider his condition too hard, when he finds himself obliged to struggle for the preservation of such a noble and powerful virtue. God never imposes on His creatures a burden which they cannot bear. However great the weakness of our fallen nature may be, the grace of Jesus Christ is superabundantly placed at our disposal, to equalize our forces in the light. We shall not be tried above our strength: the justice and goodness of God are our vouchers for this. The temptations, to which we may be subjected should not make us dejected or faint-hearted; they should rather animate us to strive after a virtue against which Satan manifests such relentless fury.

It is incumbent on every man to preserve continence according to his state and to live in the esteem of a virtue so beautiful and so necessary that its violation suffices to plunge him into the lowest, most vile state; to ruin the powers of his body; to blindfold his reason; to instigate him to trample under foot even the most sacred obligations. But our Lord, who came for the complete restoration of human nature, has graciously inspired us to pursue a higher way, where holy purity not only serves to maintain his purity and to save him from (hiSOl(l(1, Imimi, likewise, raises him from his lowly e()ll(hilioIl and unites him with God. Blessed is the man who comprehends and tastes the sweetness of this word; who could add to the renunciation of earthly goods the absolute renunciation of even those sensual pleasures which are lawful and sanctioned by an august sacrament, in a lower calling, by reason of the end that accompanies them. Blessed is he to whom it has been given by divine grace to choose, in this life, the state which all the elect enjoy in the heavenly fatherland, where, as our Lord tells us, we shall be like angels!

Perfect continency, embraced by man with the intention of complying with the second counsel of our Lord, seeks to establish in man a new degree of resemnblallce to his divine model. It includes a sacrifice time homage of which is received by God with particular satisfaction. It obliterates that division in which consists, according t:o St. Paul, the relative imperfection of the most holy marriage. It is the occasion of aim eter mu bond with God, which imprints omi lime entire person an indelible mark of glory that merits for him from God a love not be stowed on others. It reserves for God not only inanimate objects, as religious poverty does, but the hunuan creature, which there upon enters into a contract with God, as time spouse with the bridegroom. It is a state of liberty, in regard to the senses, which it purifies and sanctifies; it is the sweet scent ol- the earth, which freely mingles with that of heaven; it is an object of reverence on the part of the most worldly men, so that the heathen nations of old could not refrain from bowing down before it in homage.

Conceiving such sublime notions of religious chastity, let us always bear in mind that this virtue vowed by the religious soul is prized so dearly that its slightest infraction must necessarily be a grave offense against God. Even time lowest degree of this virtue is accompanied by immense merit. A trans formation takes place in the entire person. United to God by the most sacred contract with which He ever favoured man, fidelity is the first duty of the favoured soul. Hence, not only the breaking of this bond would be a fearful sacrilege, but every mortal or venial sin which would inculpate, in this matter of impurity, a man not bound to God by the holy vows would involve, on the part of the unfaithful religious, also the malice of sacrilege, corresponding to the enormity of the fault, just as every violation of conjugal fidelity is tainted with time malice of adultery.

Take care, therefore, to temper with holy fear the just enthusiasm which ought to be stirred in you by this sublime engagement, a contract according to which you will share the life of the angels. Humbly aspiring to the consummation of this bond which shall attach you to God forever, inquire diligently into the various means by which you may be able to fulfil it with honour and fidelity.

The first means is to realize during your whole life and under all circumstances that, in his fallen state, man cannot, by his own efforts obtain and preserve the heavenly gift of chastity, but that God alone can bestow it upon us and preserve it in us. Therefore, we must incessantly call to our assistance the divine help, asking our Lord with confidence graciously to extend His powerful hand over us, and we must redouble our entreaties at the rising wind of temptation. Very conducive to the attaimnent of chastity is recourse to Mary, because she has received the special prerogative of aiding those who faithfully defend a virtue of which she is, before all other creatures, the most perfect and magnificent expression, being styled by the Church the "Virgin of virgins." Of great help also is devotion to the holy angels, to St. Joseph, to our holy Patriarch and to time Saints of both sexes who have preserved unspotted the lily of virginal pu rity.

The second means consists in the frequent reception of the Holy Eucharist. Being the most pure body of the Incarnate Son of God, it has the special virtue of abating the rebellion of the flesh. In as much as this august sacrament transforms man in Jesus Christ, it speedily weakens concupiscence, spiritualizes the cravings of the heart, enlightens the intellect and plants in the soul a perception of the sanctity of God together with the desire of following this sanctity as a norm. Repulsed by his enemy, the devil flees from him, and if he does not yield completely at first, he nevertheless knows that his empire is threatened and in time withdraws altogether from a soul which worthily and frequently has recourse to such a powerful remedy.

The third means consists in the preservation and gradual development of the spirit of faith, which continually places before our mind, the salutary truths revealed by the merciful God. He who is ever conscious of the bounty of God manifested to man in the mysteries of the Incarnation and Redemption; he who can form for himself a true estimate of sanctifying grace which assures him the eternal possession of God; he who trembles at the thought of judgment and hell, — such a one has nothing to fear. Fl miii lv established on the rock of faith, he shall not be hurled down by temptation; very often it will attack him wjthout being able to move him at all.

The fourth means consists in loving and practising humility. God has established a mysterious relation between humility and chastity; Satan has set up a similar one between pride and impurity. This observation was made long ago by the masters of the spiritual life, and constant experience proves it very true. Always be humble and it will then be easy for yOU to remain chaste. When labouring under temptation, accept humiliations with courage, seek them and impOse them on yourselves, and you will feel, before long, that Satan's power over you is broken and that the tempest is succeeded by a calm.

The fifth means is a sincere delicacy of conscience, which takes alarm at whatsoever may menace holy chastity, whether it be in the senses or in the imagination. This delicacy, based on faithfulness and not on scrupulosity or narrow-mindedness, notes the slightest motion on the part of the enemy and is never easy as to his intentions, which are as treacherous as they are hostile. It recognizes the weak points in its line of defence and watches them most closely. A slight warning, a wound, however insignificant, is enough to prompt constant vigilance at the vulnerable spot. In fine, it is on the look-out for all the illusions of a false conscience, which have been the cause of ruin for so many.

The sixth means consists in constant control of the imaginations, by checking their wantonness. Restraint and modesty of looks are absolutely necessary to everyone who wishes to practice chastity; they belong, at time same time, to time monastic decorum. The resolutions to be taken against the other senses should reach as far as experience has proved the danger to extend. As to the imagination, it is necessary to know that everything, not only what is sinful, but also what may become hurtful, must be cut off without delay, and that reveries and laziness of mind must be constantly distrusted.

The seventh means consists in the mortification of the body. Hardships voluntarily imposed on the flesh diminish its influence and check its insolence. By habitually chastising the body, we take a salutary precaution and can easily gather enough strength for a successful repulse. Be instructed by the example of our holy Patriarch, who acquired chastity by suffering. Learn to be unremitting in the practice of penance, and you shall also, in your turn, gain a sure and lasting victory over concupiscence.

The eighth means consists in the esteem and love of holy purity. Never look upon it as bondage, but as freedom. There are, no doubt, souls which God leads by the way of long and weary temptations. In this He purposes His glory and the triumph of grace. He often sends trials of this kind to prevent greater dangers which threaten these souls. He keeps them, thereby, in humility and opens to them an immense source of merit. But this is not the way of God in respect to most of us. On the contrary, we know from experience that chastity, when loved and resoluteiy guarded, soon becomes easy in practice; the curbed senses are ruled without great effort; the imagination, subdued by the consideration of the teachings of faith, no longer goes astray; the purified heart seeks God in simplicity and finds Him. Gloomy solicitude about chastity is often more hurtful than beneficial. Prove yourselves simple and upright in this and the other points, and you shall find peace and joy for your souls.

3. Religious Obedience.

The third and most excellent of the evangelical counsels is holy obedience. It consists in the renunciation of one's own will in order to do the will of a superior, to whom one is voluntarily subject for the purpose of pleasing God. Religious obedience, therefore, differs greatly from that which is due to parents or imposed by nature, and still more from that of the soldier, which need be exterior only and still suffice. Religious obedience must be interior and directly willed, as proceeding from the free choice which the religious makes of this virtue in order to please God. Man parts, by religious poverty, from things that are not his own that he may march towards God with a lighter step; by religious chastity, he restricts the rights over his person, in order to draw near to Him; by religious obedience, however, he lays down his whole self, renouncing his will, which indeed was limited by poverty and chastity, but remained otherwise still free. This surrender is made into the hands of God, to whom the religious henceforth belongs, not only as creature, but also as a freely offered and consecrated holocaust. From that moment, there exists a contract between God and the religious soul, in virtue of which it substitutes the will of God for its own. And since God does not manifest His commands in a visible manner, but, on the contrary, wills to nourish love in the religious soul by faith, it seeks and finds His will in the creature to whom it is subjected. This, then, is the reason why such a soul attains union with God and is established in the way of perfect charity. There cannot exist a bond between two intelligent and free beings more intimate than that which is the effect of the fusion of their two distinct wills into one. Happy, therefore, the soul to whom it has been given by divine grace to understand the ineffable gain of renunciation!

Our Lord has realized this perfect obedience in His own sacred humanity. It is the underlying characteristic of His whole mortal career and is not less essential to the religious in whom Jesus Christ wishes to produce His imitation. The Son of God descended from heaven, according to His own testimony, "to do the will of His Father." He teaches us in another place (St. John iv, 34.) that the accomplishment of His divine will is His nourishment, that to fulfil it He became "obedient unto death: even to the death of the cross." (Philippians ii, 8.)

Nothing is more glorious, nothing more salutary to the soul, than obedience after the example of Jesus Christ. Sin is our greatest enemy, because it can deprive us of God. Now, sin is the product of self-will. This will, therefore, being chained down so it can not move but for a good end, is it not evident that sin is expelled from our lives wherever this blessed obedience reigns supreme. And every human and obnoxious element of the will being annihilated, is it not likewise evident that this virtue unites the soul with the will of God, which is always holy and favourably disposed towards our true interests? Thus the word of our Saviour is accomplished, who bids us to hate even our own souls, that is, our self-will; to detach ourselves from it, if we wish to serve Him in safety and be intimately attached to him.

Convinced of this truth, let us entertain true love for this virtue of obedience, which is fraught with many advantages. Let us love it as our glory; let us love it as the principle of our safety. But to practise it perseveringly, we must understand that, above all things, the spirit of faith is absolutely necessary. Faith alone can disclose to us the will of God through the person and the commands of the superior. Live, therefore, by faith and rise above that which is of flesh and blood; obey with joy and perseverance, and your obedience will be acceptable to God.

Take care to accustom yourselves, from the very beginning, never to question a command, but simply to carry it out as if you had heard the direct voice of God, being filled with thankfulness for the care He graciously takes in leading you. Should the command disagree with your own ideas, master your reason and carry out the command, from time motive that it comes from God. Beware of criticising, even interiorly, much less exteriorly, the injunctions received; for this is an unmistakable sign that the spirit of faith has deserted you, that you have become again men of the flesh.

Your obedience should be prompt, courageous and unhesitating. It should not see the difficulties and should overcome all repugnances. Nothing is more delightful to the heart of God than the spectacle of this abandonment, which is proof of the trust and love placed in Him by His creature. Neither need we be astonished at the miracles oftentimes wrought by obedience. Its effect being the concurrence of the will of God with that of the creature, in the same action, is there any thing astonishing in this, that God should work where nothing retards His action?

With this sublime precept of renunciation, which is pointed out in the holy Gospel as the indispensable way to perfection, constantly before your eyes, stand ready for any thing, awaiting only the signal in order to do on the instant the reverse of what you have done the moment before. Accomplish, with the same good will, this or that, assured that it does not matter what particular thing we do, if we only do it in accordance with the good pleasure of God, who reveals what is agreeable to Himself and will reward eternally the slightest proof of abnegation offered to Him in this world.

Fear, above all, to influence the command by showing in your manner of obeying a lack of generosity. If the Superior, upon experiencing their want of zeal, should think it necessary to spare some more than others, let such forbearance be considered one of the greatest evils that could befall them. But they should humble themselves before God for having deserved this sad privilege and allow themselves no rest until they have reconquered the right of being tried, like their brethren, in this most essential virtue of the religious.

Be most careful not to be guilty of sloth in the province of obedience; sloth, into which such fall as are not generous of heart. This consists in resting content in the enjoyment of self-will and in finding a peculiar delight in the thought that one does what he desires, there being no command to disturb his independence. Often reflect on the words of the Following of Christ: "Qui se subtrahit ab obedientia, ipse so subtrahit a gratia." Under the exercise of obedience, grace extends its empire over the soul, and merits increase and multiply; in the absence of command, the soul is very liable to lose what it has acquired, if it does not take the precaution to preserve, in good condition, that inner recollection which keeps it, day and night, disposed for grace. Often examine yourselves on this point, and may the desire of remaining for ever united with God live constantly in you, and maintain the spirit of a virtue which is the vital principle of any religious calling.

Be also on your guard against a danger to which your obedience may oftentimes be exposed by neglecting to watch most energetically over your inmost disposition. This danger is obedience, not from love of God, but from a human attraction towards the one who issues the command. It is an undeniable fact that God very often renders obedience easier to religious by infusing in them affection for their superiors. We must, however, preserving it in its entirety, strive to elevate and purify this laudable sentiment, so that the prevailing motive for the action still remains supernatural and merits for us the reward which God has stored up for us. In such instances, imagine yourselves under the obedience of a superior for whom you have no affection of this kind, and then make the resolution to obey with no less fidelity. You will acquire thereby that indifference which is as holy as it is necessary to every religious, and find yourselves equally prepared to see what you desire refused or granted, having only this end in view, that you behold in the command the holy will of God and accomplish it with willingness and determination.

Love of this virtue of obedience will render you docile not only to the will of the Superior under whose authority God has placed you, but will also put you at the disposal of those charged with your guidance or make you ready to engage in the different offices of the novitiate or the monastery. More than this, be zealous in conforming yourselves to the prescription laid down in the holy Rule (Chap. 71, where our holy Patriarch formally enjoins the brethren to be obedient to one another, that self-will be destroyed every where and the spirit of obedience, which should redress every wrong of self-will, be ever augumented in his children.

Esteeming in accordance with its great importance this fundamental spirit of the religious state, ask the Lord with fervour to avert from us, during our whole lives, that unhappy tendency which has hindered the rapid progress of more than one religious soul; we mean the practice of deliberating as to how far one violates his conscience by resisting the mandate of obedience, and hesitating only at the fear of formal sin. Unless such souls be converted, they will never reach the perfection which they have avowed. To please God, obedience must be the fruit of the liberty of a soul, devoid of selfishness, and not the result of speculative calculation. To reduce one's life to the abhorrence of formal sin, instead of seeking and doing good for its own sake, does this not mean to make one's self a base hireling of God when he could be His child; to deprive God of a glory which He expects in return for the sublime vocation to which He has called the religious soul; to constrain the heart when, on the contrary, it ought be dilated by the sentiment of love which finds its most noble and complete expression in perfect obedience?

Let us add, in conclusion, that the vows of poverty and chastity, which must necessarily be practised by the religious until death, are placed under the safeguard of obedience. He who is not obedient from the heart, will not hesitate to infringe upon poverty, whose sacrifices greatly depend on the will. How can such a one have the assurance of preserving holy chastity for any length Of time, if, in the first place, he will not listen to the counsels and injunctions of obedience, which tend to protect him against his weakness?

From all this we are to infer that obedience is the most precious gift for the religious; a treasure which he cannot love too ardently, nor defend with too much energy. It puts him in complete possession of that liberty which is enjoyed by the children of God and offered to him, even in this world — a liberty which will merit infinite glory for all eternity.

Printed in Great Britain
by Amazon

12848620R10036